U.S. PRESIDENTS

Erin Palmer

ROurke
Educational Media
rourkeeducationalmedia.com

How Are U.S. Presidents Elected?

When the nation's founders couldn't agree if a president should be elected by the popular vote of citizens or by Congress, they decided to compromise! They came up with a process called the electoral college. With the electoral college system, when a citizen casts a vote for president, they are really voting to select electors who will vote for the candidate with the most votes in the state. Each state's number of electors is equal to its number of senators and representatives in Congress. The District of Columbia has three electors and is treated like a state in the electoral college.

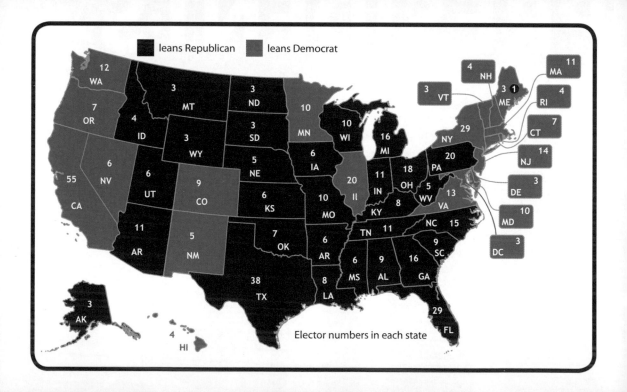

leans Republican   leans Democrat

Elector numbers in each state

There are 538 electors in all. At least 270 electoral votes are required to elect a president. Sometimes a presidential candidate wins the popular vote, but loses the electoral college! So far, it's happened five times in U.S. history. The most recent was in 2016, when Hillary Clinton got almost 2.9 million more total votes than Donald Trump, but only received 232 electoral college votes. Trump lost the popular vote, but won the presidency with 302 electoral college votes.

Table of Contents

The presidential election is held every four years on the Tuesday after the first Monday in November. Why? Farming! When an official voting day was chosen in 1845, many people worked as farmers and lived far from their polling place. A Tuesday allowed people Monday for travel. November was chosen because it was after the harvest was complete, and before the harsh winter weather set in.

THE WHAT HOUSE?

From the pages of history books to the faces on dollar bills, United States presidents are a huge part of American **culture**. Though it's a serious job, plenty of silly and surprising things go on behind the White House doors!

George Washington
(1732–1799)

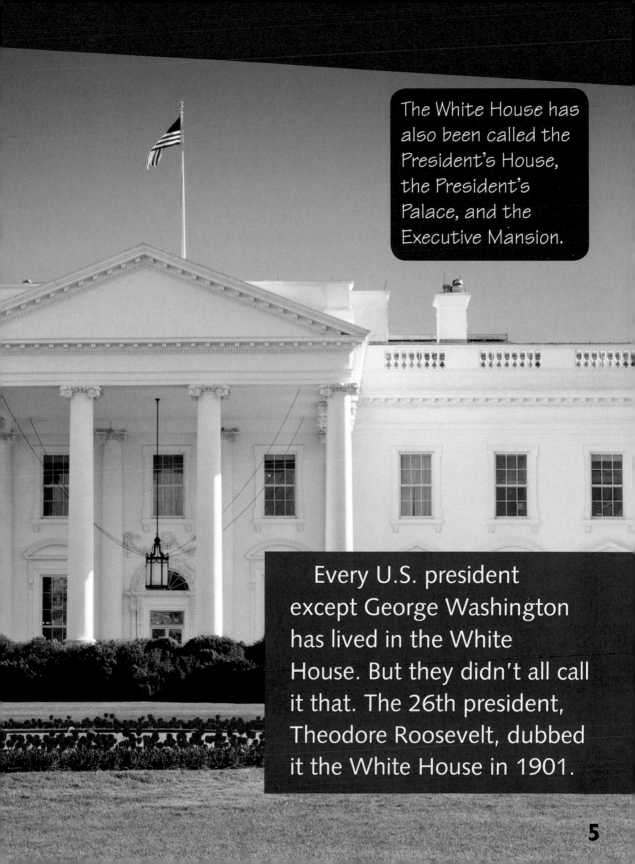

The White House has also been called the President's House, the President's Palace, and the Executive Mansion.

Every U.S. president except George Washington has lived in the White House. But they didn't all call it that. The 26th president, Theodore Roosevelt, dubbed it the White House in 1901.

Perplexing Presidential Pets

Roosevelt didn't just name the White House. He also filled it with pets, including cats, dogs, birds, snakes, guinea pigs, and a badger!

Giddy Up the Elevator!
Theodore Roosevelt's son Quentin once brought the family's pony into the White House and up the elevator to cheer up his sick brother.

Unusual pets were part of many presidential families. Herbert Hoover had a pet possum. Calvin Coolidge had a pet raccoon. Rebecca the raccoon walked through the White House on a leash.

Sometimes leaders from other nations gave U.S. presidents **extraordinary** pets as gifts. The King of Siam (now Thailand) gave President James Buchanan a herd of elephants.

President Martin Van Buren received tiger cubs from the Sultan of Oman. President John Quincy Adams got an alligator from the Marquis de Lafayette. The gator lived in a bathroom in the White House. Yikes!

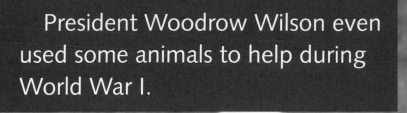

President Woodrow Wilson even used some animals to help during World War I.

Ruff Life

Warren Harding loved his dog so much that he threw Laddie Boy a doggy birthday party at the White House. Other dogs came and they enjoyed a frosted cake made from dog biscuits.

Wilson brought in a herd of sheep to eat the grass on the White House lawn. This kept the grass trimmed when it was difficult to find workers.

Ronald Reagan
(1911–2004)

Jobs, Fashion, and Facial Hair

Many presidents held **fascinating** jobs before taking office. The 39th president, Jimmy Carter, was a peanut farmer. The 40th president, Ronald Reagan, was an actor.

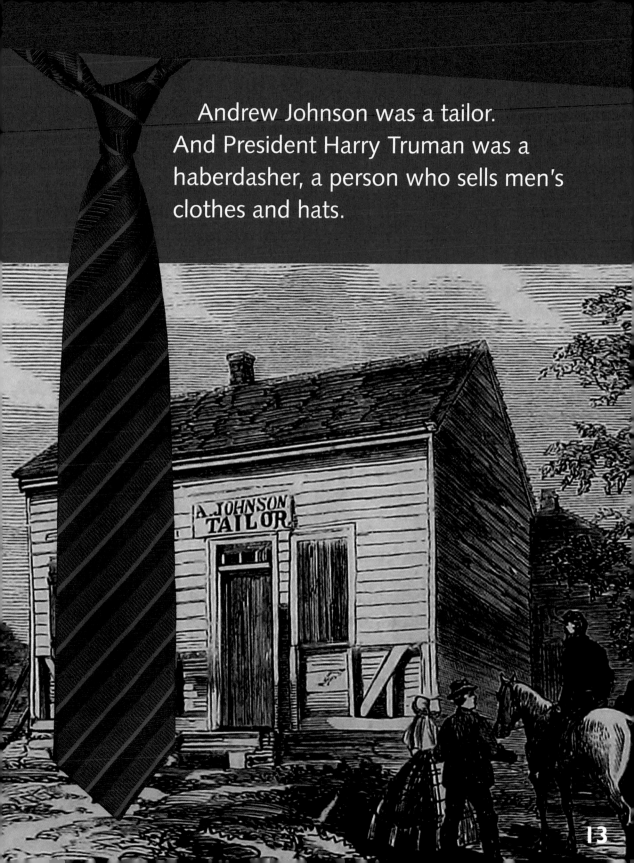

Andrew Johnson was a tailor. And President Harry Truman was a haberdasher, a person who sells men's clothes and hats.

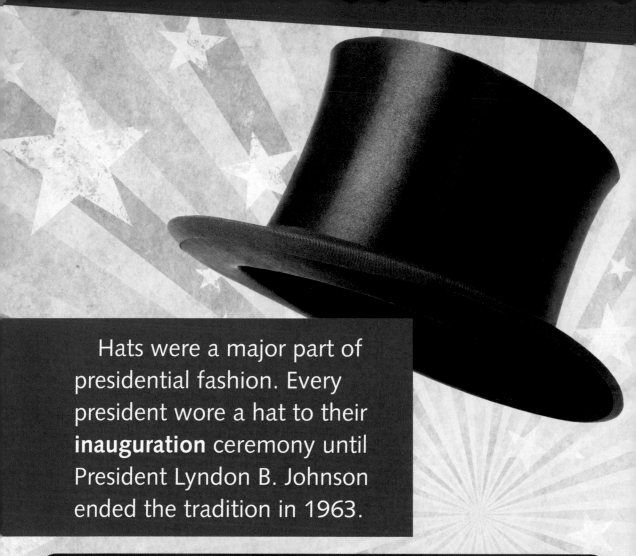

Hats were a major part of presidential fashion. Every president wore a hat to their **inauguration** ceremony until President Lyndon B. Johnson ended the tradition in 1963.

Hat's Off!

This tradition came to a sad end with Lyndon B. Johnson's unusual inauguration. He took the oath of office aboard Air Force One at Love Field Airport following the assassination of John F. Kennedy.

Lyndon B. Johnson (1908–1973)

John F. Kennedy (right), and his father, Joseph Kennedy, wear top hats at JFK's inauguration January 20, 1961.

John F. Kennedy (1917–1963)

Joseph Kennedy (1888–1969)

Though many presidents wore hats,
there is one that stood out among the rest.
Abraham Lincoln's hats were quite famous!
He even stored important papers in them.

Heads Above the Rest
Lincoln's grand hats made him appear even taller, but he didn't need the extra height. Abraham Lincoln loomed largest of all the presidents at six feet, four inches (193 centimeters) tall.

His hats were not the only fashion choice that made Lincoln **unique**. He was also the first president to have a beard!

Abraham Lincoln
(1809–1865)

I Mustache You ...
Only nine presidents have had beards or mustaches, though some did have some serious sideburns!

17

Presidential Firsts and Quirks

Speaking of firsts …
Theodore Roosevelt was the first president to ride in a car in 1902. He was also the first president to ride in a submarine. He loved adventure!

Theodore Roosevelt
(1858–1919)

Tweet

Home

@ Connect

Discover

Me

Barack Obama ✓
@BarackObama

Four more years. pic.twitter.com/bAJE6Vom
7/11/12 12:16 PTG

From flying to tweeting, here are some other presidential firsts:

- First president to ride in an airplane while in office: Franklin Delano Roosevelt
- First to have a telephone in the White House: Rutherford B. Hayes in 1877
- First president to have a website for the White House: Bill Clinton in 1994
- First president to use social media to connect with everyday Americans: Barack Obama

U.S. presidents have had many interesting nicknames, from the "Human Iceberg" (Benjamin Harrison) to "Elegant Arthur" (Chester A. Arthur).

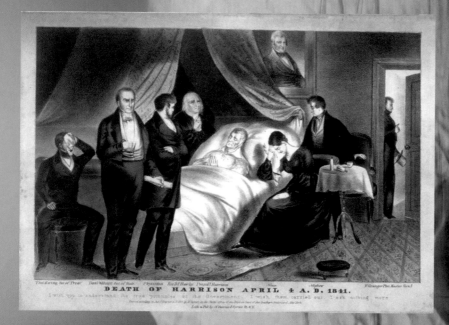

DEATH OF HARRISON APRIL 4 A. D. 1841.

William Henry Harrison (1773–1841), Benjamin's grandfather, was also president. But only president for a month. He became ill and died 31 days into his presidency.

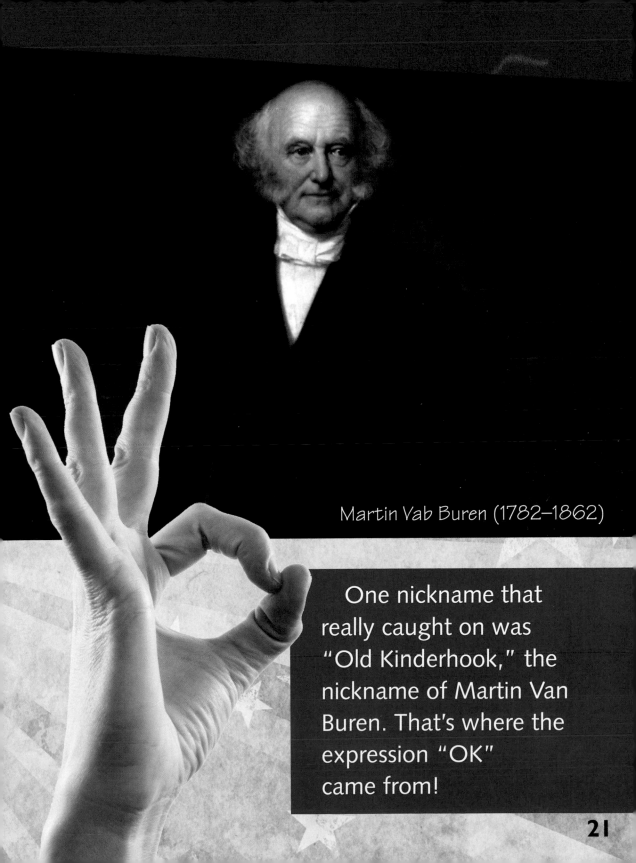

Martin Vab Buren (1782–1862)

One nickname that really caught on was "Old Kinderhook," the nickname of Martin Van Buren. That's where the expression "OK" came from!

Another nickname that lasted long after his presidency is from Theodore "Teddy" Roosevelt. A toymaker created the first "Teddy Bear" stuffed animal to honor the president!

Theodore Roosevelt

Teddy bears became so popular that toymakers tried to do the same thing to honor William H. Taft. However, the "Billy Possum" toy did not catch on.

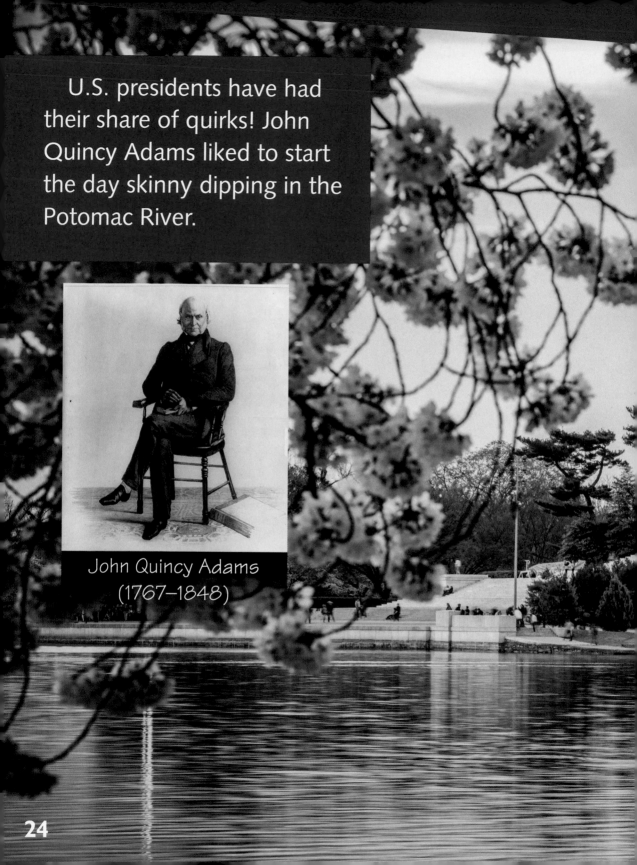

U.S. presidents have had their share of quirks! John Quincy Adams liked to start the day skinny dipping in the Potomac River.

John Quincy Adams
(1767–1848)

His naked swims were no secret. A reporter once used the morning **ritual** to get an interview with the president. She sat on his clothes until he agreed!

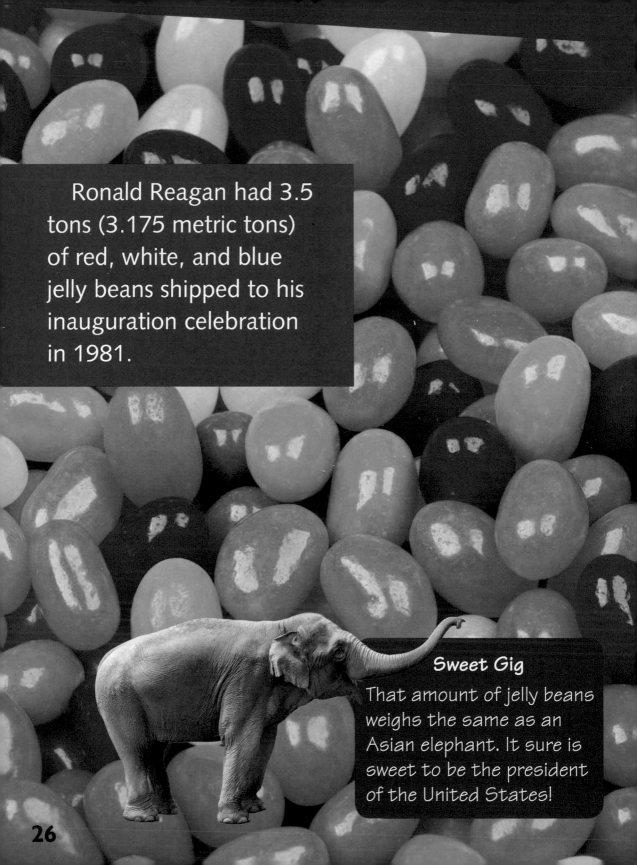

Ronald Reagan had 3.5 tons (3.175 metric tons) of red, white, and blue jelly beans shipped to his inauguration celebration in 1981.

Sweet Gig

That amount of jelly beans weighs the same as an Asian elephant. It sure is sweet to be the president of the United States!

Reagan loved jelly beans so much that he had them delivered to the White House throughout his entire presidency.

Ronald Reagan

More...Really Weird, True Facts!

Theodore Roosevelt and Franklin D. Roosevelt were fifth cousins.

Rumor has it that Andrew Jackson taught his pet parrot how to curse.

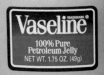

Calvin Coolidge had someone rub Vaseline on his head every morning while he ate breakfast. Weird!

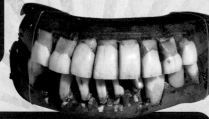

John Adams and Thomas Jefferson died on the same day, July 4, 1826, the 50th anniversary of the Declaration of Independence.

George Washington's fake teeth were made of hippopotamus ivory, bone, animal and human teeth, lead, brass screws, and gold wire.

James Monroe died on July 4th, 1831, 55 years after the Declaration of Independence was signed.

James Madison is the smallest president to date. He was five feet, four inches (1.63 meters) tall and weighed about 100 pounds (45 kilograms).

ΕΝΗΡΖΡΕΓΧ
ΩΔΖΛΝ ΜΝ

According to legend, James A. Garfield could write in Greek with one hand and Latin with the other—at the same time!

William Henry Harrison was the first president to have electricity in the White House. And he was terrified of being electrocuted. It's said that he refused to touch the light switches and slept with all the lights on!

After his father died, Andrew Johnson's mother sent him to be an indentured servant for a tailor. He later made all his own suits as president.

Abraham Lincoln was a wrestler—a really good one! He only lost one match in twelve years.

Index

Glossary

culture (KUHL-chur): the ideas, customs, traditions, and way of life of a group of people

extraordinary (ek-STROR-duh-ner-ee): very unusual or impressive

fascinating (FAS-uh-nate-ing): to attract or hold the attention of

inauguration (in-aw-gyuh-RAY-shun): the ceremony of swearing in a public official

ritual (rich-ew-uhl): an act or series of acts regulary repeated in a set precise manner

unique (yoo-NEEK): unlike anything else

Show What You Know

1. How did a reporter get an interview with John Quincy Adams?
2. What candy did Ronald Reagan love?
3. Where did the expression "OK" come from?
4. Who was the first president to ride in a submarine?
5. Who is the tallest U.S. president (so far!)?

Websites to Visit

www.kids.usa.gov/government/presidents

www.mrnussbaum.com/presidents

www.usa4kids.com/presidents

About the Author

Erin Palmer is a writer in Tampa, Florida. She loves to travel, try new foods and go to the beach. Erin has a lot of nieces and nephews, which is why she loves to write children's books. Her whole huge family loves to read! Erin has written a variety of fiction and nonfiction books for kids. And guess what? A weird, true fact about Erin is that she laughs a lot, especially when it's really quiet!

Meet The Author!
www.meetREMauthors.com

www.rourkeeducationalmedia.com

PHOTO CREDITS: Cover and title page: ©mammoth, ©fotoslaz, ©mayakova, ©P_Wei, ©Library of Congress, ©TokenPhoto; table of contents: ©geniebird; p.4: ©Classix; p.5: ©OlegAlbinsky; p.6-7: ©GlobalP (cat, snake, dog), ©Eric Isselée (guinea pig, raccoon, parrot), ©Karel Broz (badger); p.8: ©hatman12 (ribbon), ©Donovan van Staden; p.9: ©aleks223 (clipart), ©Alan Kaewkhammul; p.10-11: ©FabioFilzi; p.13: ©taseffski (tie); p.14: ©art-4-art; p.16: ©madebymacro (clipart); p.16, 17, 18: ©Everett Historial; p.19: ©AHMAD FAIZAL YAHYA, ©tapui (plane); p.20: ©Niyazz; p.21, 23: ©Library of Congress; p.21: ©BravissimoS; p22-23: ©Ivonne Wierink; p.24-25: ©SeanPavonePhoto; p.26: ©dndavis, ©craftvision (elephant); p.27: ©mark reistein/Alamy Stock Photo; p.27: ©camilla wisbauer (petroleum jelly), Courtesy of Mount Vernon Ladies' Association (teeth), ©MaryValery (tombstone); p.28: ©BlueSkyImage; all other photos Public Domain

Edited by: Keli Sipperley
Cover design by: Tara Raymo
Interior design by: Rhea Magaro-Wallace

Library of Congress PCN Data

U.S. Presidents / Erin Palmer
(Weird, True Facts)
ISBN 978-1-68342-367-6 (hard cover)
ISBN 978-1-68342-533-5 (e-Book)
Library of Congress Control Number: 2017931259

Rourke Educational Media
Printed in the United States of America,
North Mankato, Minnesota